PLAYFUL PANEL QUILTS

Surprising Settings · Stunning Results

CYNDI MCCHESNEY

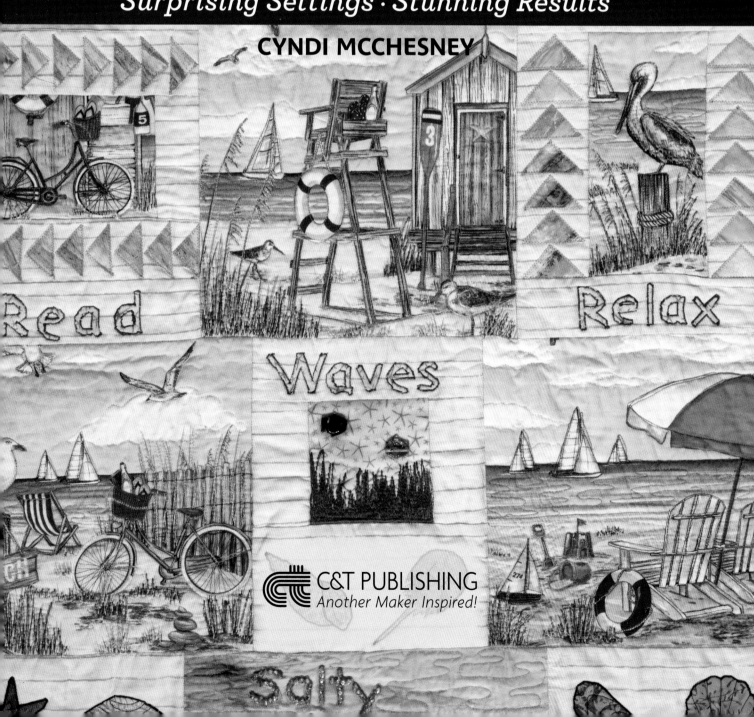

C&T PUBLISHING
Another Maker Inspired!

Text copyright © 2024 by Cynthia Ann McChesney

Photography and artwork copyright © 2024 by C&T Publishing, Inc.

Publisher: Amy Barrett-Daffin

Creative Director: Gailen Runge

Senior Editor: Roxane Cerda

Technical Editor: Helen Frost

Cover/Book Designer: April Mostek

Production Coordinator: Tim Manibusan

Illustrator: Kirstie L. Petterson

Photography by C&T Publishing, unless otherwise noted

Published by C&T Publishing, Inc., P.O. Box 1456, Lafayette, CA 94549

Library of Congress Cataloging-in-Publication Data

Names: McChesney, Cyndi, 1955- author.

Title: Playful panel quilts : surprising settings, stunning results / Cyndi McChesney.

Description: Lafayette, CA : C&T Publishing, [2024] | Summary: "Building off of Cyndi McChesney's first panel book, this book takes the concept of designing panel quilts to the next level. From creating small freeform quilts to working panels into traditional whole quilt settings and row-by-row quilts using panels, quilters will learn how to make their panels shine"-- Provided by publisher.

Identifiers: LCCN 2023050910 | ISBN 9781644035030 (trade paperback) | ISBN 9781644035047 (ebook)

Subjects: LCSH: Patchwork--Patterns. | Quilting--Patterns. | BISAC: CRAFTS & HOBBIES / Patchwork | CRAFTS & HOBBIES / Sewing

Classification: LCC TT835 .M2375 2024 | DDC 746.46--dc23/eng/20231201

LC record available at https://lccn.loc.gov/2023050910

Printed in China

10 9 8 7 6 5 4 3 2 1

DEDICATION

My quilting friends, Pat Greenberg and Martha Powers-Nosal, encouraged me for years to write a book—I did, and then I wrote this one! Thank you to you two ladies for all of your love and support. AND thanks to all the students and quilt contributors for continuing to participate in my classes and pushing me to try new things as well as answering more "what-if" questions—none of this would be possible without all of you!

ACKNOWLEDGMENTS

The team at C&T Publishing is amazing, and their encouragement is invaluable: I appreciate all of you! Thank you for the many ideas, tools, suggestions, and cheerleading! You are the best!

My personal quilts are designed, constructed, and quilted by me. My go-to supplies include Aurifl 50-weight two-ply thread for piecing, Quilters Dream Batting, and Signature 40-weight cotton quilting thread for the quilting. I look for panels everywhere. Many thanks to all the fabric manufacturers that keep supplying us with fun and innovative panels.

CONTENTS

FOREWORD

There is nothing more fun than exploring creativity and coming up with original results, but not everyone is secure in starting from nothing. I have always encouraged originality in my students. Many of my own books are meant to be kickstarters rather than a collection of complete, ready-to-make patterns. In most cases, quilters fare best when given a nudge in the right direction and this book does just that!

Playful Panel Quilts provides tools, tips, and tricks that will spark that creative journey and lead you to make a fun, one-of-a-kind, and personalized quilt. Cyndi categorizes various approaches to the design layout possibilities and outlines a variety of ways to use the amazing panels and photo fabrics available to us these days. The use of panel fabrics allows for additional bold impact without time-consuming fuss—but the end results are just as grand! As a cheerleader for creativity, I personally am excited that you have this book in your hands and are about to embark on a thrilling and rewarding journey.

— Ricky Tims

INTRODUCTION

Following the release of my first book, *Fun with Panels* (C&T Publishing, 2022), students began to ask for more instruction on some of the styles of panel quilts from the book's gallery. As a result, I decided to delve more deeply into the nitty-gritty of how I designed those quilts and share that information with you!

With a focus on multi-image panels, we'll explore traditional and innovative settings. You'll find specifics on creating your own traditionally pieced and foundation-pieced blocks, along with tips for creating appliqué patterns and all the math you'll need to achieve a successful and stunning quilt.

Although this is not a project-based book, you will find lots of step-by-step information on designing panel quilts using repeated block settings, row-by-row designs, and small art-style or montage quilts. You'll find detailed instructions for designing your own appliquéd and pieced blocks, and so much more.

I hope you'll join me in creating a one-of-a-kind panel quilt beyond any panel quilt you've imagined before. Grab a panel, and let's have fun!

QUILT STYLES *and* SETTINGS *for* MULTI-IMAGE PANELS

Panels offer an incredibly rich palette for us as quilters! Unlike an artist with a blank canvas, who has to determine style, medium, color palette, subject, and so forth, we are blessed with a terrific jumping-off place provided by whatever panel we select!

The subject matter, the color palette, and, to some degree, even the style are hinted at within the panel itself. All you have to do is look around and let your panel guide you! The information you seek is all right there—it's just a matter of thoroughly observing and interpreting what you see.

In this chapter, we'll take an in-depth look at several approaches that lend themselves wonderfully to panels that feature multiple images. Panels come in a variety of styles, from solo panels (a single image), to panels with multiple same-size images, to panels with images of various shapes and sizes. Each style lends itself to endless opportunities for designing unique, original, and imaginative quilt projects.

REPEAT BLOCK DESIGNS

It helps to have a little familiarity with some of the different types of quilts or traditional quilt settings as a jumping-off point. If you're not sure where to start, consider the different settings presented in the following pages and see which speaks to you as you begin to create your own unique quilt.

For those wishing to dip your toes cautiously into the design pool, take a look at these tools from C&T Publishing that could help you identify quilt settings with an open space in a repeated pattern where panel images can be highlighted:

The New Ladies' Art Company Quick & Easy Block Tool, by Connie Chunn

The New Quick & Easy Block Tool

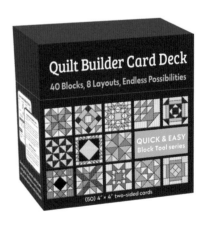

Quilt Builder Card Deck

Once you've selected a traditional block that, when repeated, provides a setting where you can highlight your panel images, you'll need some basic skills to make the process simple and fun.

Numerous quilt patterns offer options for using a panel in this manner. For more examples, check out the quilts in the Gallery of Quilts (page 49)!

Down on the Bunny Farm, 38˝ × 47˝ Repeated Block quilt by the author
Bunny Tails continuous blocks panel by Robert Giordano for Henry Glass & Co., Inc.

This quilt was created by the author, using the Country Farm block.
The block has a large open space that is a perfect platform in which to feature these adorable bunnies.

ROW-BY-ROW QUILTS USING PANELS

Another fun and creative option for highlighting panel images is the style of the popular row-by-row quilt. What is a row-by-row quilt? Row-by-row quilts are made of rows of quilt blocks or components, but each row is distinct from the others. This quilt style was made popular in 2013 by Janet Lutz's Row by Row Experience, a quilt shop-hop collaboration.

Once again, your panel will provide you with everything you need to create a unique and imaginative row-by-row quilt. When you use a panel as the starting point, this version or interpretation of a traditional row-by-row quilt relies a bit more on your ability to gather the themes from your panel and, most importantly, to correctly do all the math. You must consider several elements as you embark on creating a row-by-row quilt using a panel, and we will get into all the details later in Panels in Row-by-Row Quilts (page 18).

I find row-by-row quilts made with panels to be really exciting! As we delve into how to create your distinct rows, you'll have an opportunity to discover ways to create appliqué patterns using your panel motifs, learn how to create your own paper-pieced blocks, and find out how to graph components to enhance your design.

Love and a Dog, 63˝ × 66˝ Row-by-row quilt by the author
All You Need Is Love and a Dog panels by Beth Logan for Henry Glass & Co., Inc.

I love my dog and enjoyed coming up with block settings and theme rows to enhance the motifs of this panel.

MONTAGE WITH PANELS

Looking for more ways to play with a panel? How about an art-style quilt using a panel? Yes! Absolutely! Step way out of your comfort zone and jump into creating a montage quilt! For a step-by-step guide to creating your own special art quilt using a panel, follow along in Montage Quilts Using Panels (page 21).

A montage is a work that includes words, images, and embellishment. When it's done well, the viewer often cannot distinguish the panel from the surrounding enhancements and images! The techniques of creating appliqué patterns, paper-pieced patterns, and graphing your own blocks are all essential tools in designing one of these projects. Keep reading to discover how to create word appliqué right on your home computer, and then you'll top it all off by determining what kinds of embellishments to add.

Panels aren't just something to add borders to—you can do so much more! Be brave, be creative, and whoop it up!

The 19th Hole, 30″ × 43″ Montage quilt by Terry Helmer
Back Nine panel by Elizabeth Medley
for Blank Quilting Corporation

Terry explains, "I selected this panel because my son, Shannon, loves to play golf with friends every Sunday. He grew up living on a golf course, and his grandparents were avid golfers. I got the idea for this wall hanging as soon as Cyndi started giving her presentation to my guild. The idea 'The 19th Hole' slammed into me. Shannon works from home, and I think this wall hanging will brighten his workspace."

Many traditional quilt patterns lend themselves perfectly to highlighting multiple images in a panel. Many one- or two-block quilts feature open space where you can insert panel images. The biggest obstacles you will encounter are identifying ideal patterns and adjusting the size so that the panel images fit.

When searching for quilt designs that have open spaces, keep in mind that you can also create open space within the quilt block itself, as I discuss in detail in *Fun with Panels* (C&T Publishing, 2022).

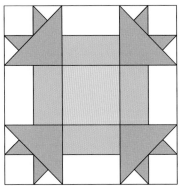

Peony Nine Patch

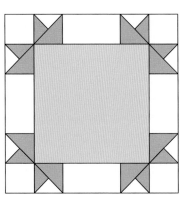

Peony Nine Patch Variation

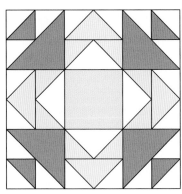

Sister's Choice

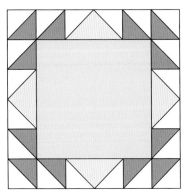

Sister's Choice Variation

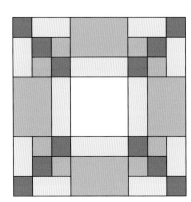

Puss in the Corner

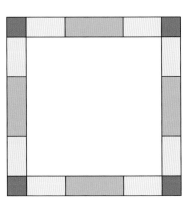

Puss in the Corner Variation

The Irish Chain quilt is a great example of this type of repeated block design. In its more straightforward and basic form, an Irish Chain quilt is simply a Nine Patch block alternating with a solid space and set apart with sashing and cornerstones. The beauty of the design is the open space that is built into it, as shown in this example of a simple Irish Chain quilt.

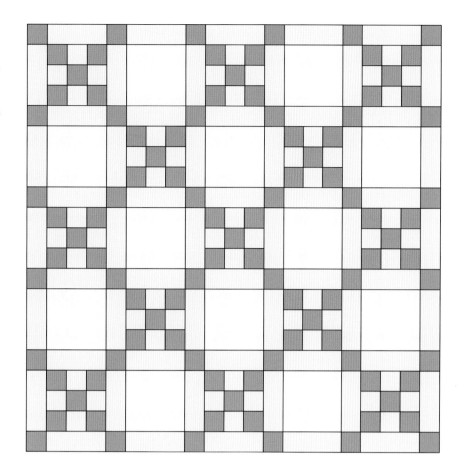

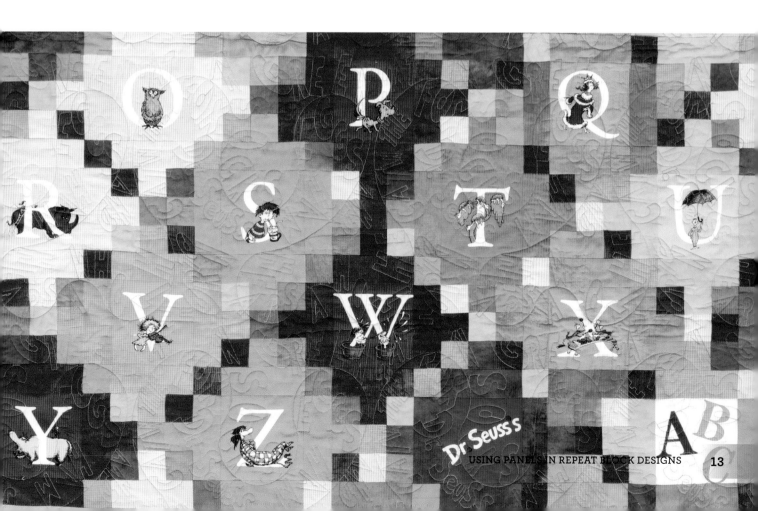

When working with panels consisting of multiple same-size images, consider a setting such as this one, in which you can highlight your panel images. With its inclusion of the Dr. Seuss's ABC panel and some hand-dyed fabrics, note how playful and whimsical this simple, scrappy Irish Chain quilt becomes. Follow along as I walk through the steps of how I made the math work for this quilt in Repeated Block Setting Quilts (page 28).

Here's an example of a block called Country Farm, which I selected to highlight the cute Easter Bunny-themed panel images in my quilt *Down on the Bunny Farm* (page 9). Any block that has a space that already exists or can be created by leaving units out and that creates a great pattern and flow when placed together will work wonderfully for this kind of setting.

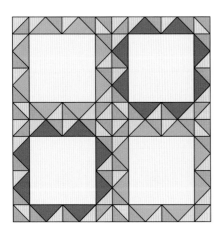

In another quilt, I used the Friendship Star block in such a manner as to create an open center space, and that's where my panel images live! View this quilt, *Circle of Friends*, in the Gallery (page 52).

Dr. Seuss's ABC Panel by Robert Kaufman Fabrics

Dr. Seuss Goes to Ireland, 52˝ × 59˝ Repeated Block quilt by the author

Irish Chain quilts are so visually appealing that using this panel and a collection of hand-dyed fabrics
by Ricky Tims seemed like a perfect fit.

STEPS TO SUCCESS USING A REPEAT BLOCK DESIGN

To successfully use a traditional quilt block to feature a panel, you'll need to follow just a few steps.

1. Select a panel with at least eight or more panel images that are all the same size **or** that can be trimmed or framed with added strips to become the same size. The number of panel images and the size of those images will guide you to determine a size for your quilt. For example, if you have only a small number of panel images, the quilt may be smaller in size. More images will allow you to add more blocks. The size of the images also affects the size of the quilt. If the panel images are large, fewer images will result in a larger quilt; if they are small, many images may still yield only a small quilt, depending on the block or setting you select.

2. Next, choose a quilt pattern with one or two blocks that you like and that you believe can accommodate and showcase the panel you are working with. Look for blocks that allow space to insert your panel images. See Resources (page 62) for a list of quilt block references every quilter's library should include!

3. Once you have identified a quilt pattern with repeated blocks that will work for your project, you'll need to determine how to size the pattern or repeated block to encompass the panel images you have. Making the measurements work is critical to the outcome of your project, but the math is so much easier than you might think. I walk you through that process step by step in Repeated Block Setting Quilts (page 28).

TRADITIONAL QUILT BLOCKS THAT WORK WITH PANELS

Here are some other examples of traditional quilt blocks that are perfect for highlighting panel images.

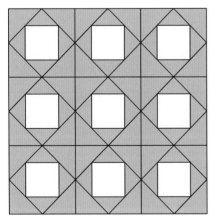

Square in a Square

Sawtooth Star

Storm at Sea

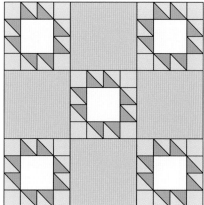

Lady of the Lake

Churn Dash

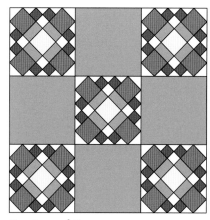

Domino and Square

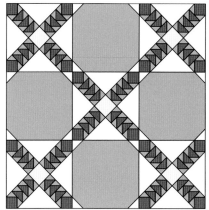

Odd Fellows

Old Tippecanoe

Toad in a Puddle

PANELS *in* ROW-BY-ROW QUILTS

Get ready to have even more fun and be sure you are wearing your playful party hat when you delve into creating a row-by-row quilt using panels. An absolute must is one or more multi-image panels with related themes. Note that I said "one or more"! If you have two multi-image panels with a similar theme and color palette, why not use them together in a row-by-row quilt?

FINDING DESIGN FEATURES

It helps to have multiple-image panels with six or more images. The more images, the bigger your quilt, and the more themes or motifs you'll find to create your additional rows. For an especially entertaining (and challenging) quilt, your panel doesn't have to have all same-size images—it helps, but it's definitely not mandatory.

For a row-by-row quilt, you will need to think of a different block for each row and consider how you will create the blocks in that row. Will they be framed panel images, pieced blocks, or appliquéd blocks?

One of the best inspiration sources for design ideas and motifs, as well as traditional quilt blocks, is your panel itself. Before beginning any panel quilt, I study the panel and let it speak to me. I place the panel in its entirety on my design wall and do quite a bit of brainstorming and jotting down of ideas. The panel holds a lot of clues as to what will complement the design. This process is also where the creative filler comes from!

For example, if my panel includes a windmill, I might jot down "pinwheels." Straight lines often remind me of Log Cabin, Rail Fence, Piano Keys, or other blocks made from strips. Flowers and suns remind me of New York Beauty or Dresden Plate blocks and other circular designs. If I'm working on a montage, I might jot down "yo-yos" as a possibility for an embellishment. Use your quilting knowledge; you know a lot about quilts and patterns, and this is where all of that experience comes into play.

Sometimes, you'll find that you have the smallest of spaces to fill, but I encourage you to dig into that list you created and see whether you can use something from that list of ideas; and remember, even the simplest half-square triangle will be far more interesting than a plain square of fabric.

Take a look at the wonderful quilts in the Gallery of Quilts (page 49) and study how each quilter found a way to use creative filler to complete the designs. Remember to stay flexible, play, don't stress yourself out, use your imagination, and have some fun!

The key to successful brainstorming is to stay open to ideas. Generate as many ideas as you can without censoring them as you go. Be as spontaneous as possible and do not discard any ideas until you are ready to start narrowing things down.

For example, when I was creating my *Love and a Dog* row-by-row quilt, I started by jotting down ideas of what I know about dogs and what I saw in the panel. I let my imagination run wild.

Perhaps the panel itself only holds one or two obvious clues, but you probably know a **lot** about dogs. Dogs are love (hearts); they enjoy chewing on bones, chasing balls, peeing on fire hydrants (sorry, but it's true), hanging out in their homes (doghouses); they generally consider themselves the king or queen of the castle; they leave muddy pawprints everywhere; and much, much more. Each of these ideas became the theme for a row within my quilt.

Some of the quotes within one of the panels also led me to specific quilt blocks I selected to highlight different images. For example, "Dogs Rule" made me think of a king or queen, which led me to use the King's Crown block variation. "The Road to My Heart Is Paved with Pawprints" gave me two more ideas for themed rows: hearts and pawprints. I had the option to photocopy the heart from the panel and enlarge it to create a heart appliqué. Instead, I went to another favorite resource, Google Images, and found a heart and a pawprint that suited the style of the quilt and created appliqué patterns from those. For more on designing your own appliquéd blocks, see Creating Your Own Appliqué Patterns (page 45).

King's Crown block variation

Detail of *Love and a Dog*, 63˝ × 67˝ Row-by-row quilt by the author
This quilt features two companion panels from Henry Glass Fabrics that have complementary themes and color schemes.

MAKING A ROW-BY-ROW QUILT WORK

Possibly the most difficult aspect of creating a row-by-row quilt is getting all the rows to work out to the same width. This task does require that you do a lot of measuring and a bit of math, but it isn't as daunting as it might seem; read on to see how to accomplish this. I walk you through all the math so your quilt turns out perfectly, as explained in Row-by-Row Quilts (page 30).

Flexibility is the key to a successful row-by-row quilt—or any panel quilt, for that matter! First and foremost, don't box yourself in by defining the outcome because you may need to juggle slightly once you get going. With that said, I do begin with a rough idea of how big I want the quilt to be (for example, 50˝ × 60˝), but I **don't set this size in stone**—at least not yet!

I graphed the doghouses to a 12˝ × 12˝ block in order to feature a 6˝ dog image within the house. Using four of them resulted in a row that measured 48˝ (finished) from edge to edge. Height is much less of a consideration when creating a row-by-row quilt; the most important measurement is the width of the rows, which ultimately all has to be the same. This row defined a measurement for me that I chose to keep when creating all the other rows. I could have waited

to see what size other rows might have become, but I liked the size produced with the 12˝ doghouses.

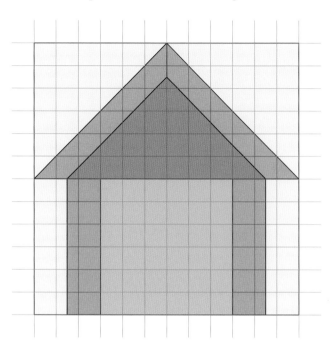

Working on graph paper, graph all of your blocks and rows to the defined width and then finish as desired. For step-by-step instructions, please see Making the Measurements Work (page 24).

MONTAGE QUILTS USING PANELS

A *montage* is defined as a work that includes words, images, and music (which I have loosely interpreted as "embellishments"). After all, what is music but an embellishment for so many works of art, such as movies, video games, and so on? For me, a montage quilt is my opportunity to stretch the definition of an art quilt to include an art quilt that begins with a panel!

I like to work with multi-image panels for my montage quilts, but your imagination might discover a way to use a solo panel for the same purpose. Once again, the panel images do not all have to be the same size. I think that a montage quilt is the perfect platform in which to incorporate a panel that has a variety of image sizes.

Creating your montage quilt begins with choosing a panel with a number of interesting images. Next, begin your brainstorming process with this panel. Make a list of words that jump out at you to describe either the theme of the montage you plan to create or images that the panel evokes.

You may want to use text appliqué to emphasize the theme. Try several different fonts because they can enhance the sense of whimsy, dreaminess, or other emotions that you wish to evoke in your piece. Create text appliqué on your personal computer, following the steps in Creating Text as Appliqué (page 47). There are additional techniques to create word appliqué, this is just the technique that I use. Explore other options!

Create a map for your project so that you are confident everything fits together and you have used interesting filler for any open spaces.

Piece, appliqué, and construct your quilt; complete the quilting; and finally, add the embellishments. Depending on the type of embellishments you use, your piece may not be machine washable when completed. Keep the function of the quilt in mind as you select your embellishments.

Follow along as I guide you through the process I used to create my *Sunflower Pastures* montage.

Sunflower Pastures 49″ × 50″ Montage quilt by the author
Sunflower Stampede panel by John Keeling for 3 Wishes Fabric

I discovered this horse-themed panel on a 2022 trip through Texas, and it brought back wonderful
memories of a beautiful Palomino mare I owned years ago. I had fun adding sunflowers, Western-themed
charms, and other embellishments to the finished quilt. It makes me smile when I look at it!

LET'S START WITH THE WORDS!

Study your panel, and as you do so, write down every word that comes to mind. It is unlikely that you will use *all* of them, but the more choices you come up with, the more interesting and diverse the finished project. I have found that sometimes the words take the quilt in an unexpected and different direction than I first imagined, and that's okay! Refer to the earlier section on brainstorming, Finding Design Features (page 18).

For my *Sunflower Pastures* quilt, I could see horses, horses running, sunflowers, barns, families, joy, happiness, and love. I love horses, and although I no longer own any of my own, there's just something special about the bond between a woman and her horse.

I chose the words "grace," "beauty," "family," "free," "joy," "love," and "I love horses." Then, I found a font I wanted to use and created my word appliqué, following the steps listed in Creating Text as Appliqué (page 47).

COLLECTING EMBELLISHMENTS

Now, it's time to begin gathering embellishments! I often save this step for last, but I sometimes do gather embellishments as I'm working on my piece. I might find interesting items at my local craft or sewing store, so when I see them, I purchase them.

Embellishments might include embroidery, buttons, beads, crystals, pins, patches, wiggly eyes, ribbons, bows, small charms, or anything that sparks your imagination and will enhance your art piece. Keep your eyes open and set aside a box or container for storing your treasures until you are ready to add them to the quilt.

I usually wait to add embellishments until the quilt is finished, but you may wish to add some types, such as embroidery, sooner. Embroidered blocks should be incorporated as you construct your quilt. Embroidered elements, such as snowflakes or flowers, can be added at any time, but consider waiting to add those until after the quilting has been completed. I prefer to add the other embellishments later so that I can do the quilting without having to maneuver around them.

MAKING *the* MEASUREMENTS WORK

Math is a four-letter word—and so is *love*! I'm hoping you will learn to *love the math* that you need to master to make your panel projects successful with the least number of headaches and problems. I want you to triumph, so taking time to love the math will ensure that you don't fold up your project and stash it away.

As any carpenter will tell you, the old adage of "measure twice, cut once" applies to quilt making as well. In the case of designing your unique panel quilts, no matter the style, I cannot emphasize enough the importance of continually checking your math! Use graph paper because a well-executed design on graph paper will eliminate most of the issues you may encounter along the way.

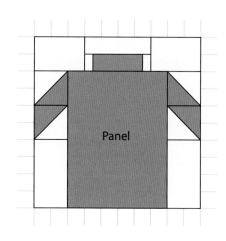

It's impractical to graph your design to full size—simply adjust your scale. Use graph paper with **4 squares to the inch**. This option makes the most sense for quilters, as we work in increments of ¼˝.

I usually design my quilts by using a scale of 1 inch per square, so 10 squares would equal 10˝. If this seems too big, downsize the scale to equal 2 inches per square. My 10˝ × 10˝ Ugly Sweater block was graphed by using one square of graph paper to equal 1 inch in real life.

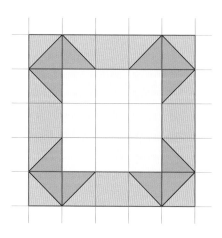

Here's an example of a block graphed by using 2 inches per square. Although the graphed block is only 5 × 5 squares, the finished block will be 10˝ × 10˝.

PREPARING PANEL IMAGES

Preparing and determining a measurement you can work with are essential to beginning to graph and using the panel images either as stand-alone images or within traditional quilt blocks.

It's important to begin with square or rectangular panel images. You've probably noticed that when you get your panel home from the quilt shop, the images are a tad wonky! I follow a number of steps to remedy this issue before I begin designing any of my panel quilts.

I always prewash my panels because I don't like working with all the chemicals on the fabric. And more importantly, I have found that prewashing the panels relaxes the fabric so that what starts off as really wonky often becomes quite a bit less wonky.

Cut the panel images apart, leaving as much space around each as possible, at least until you determine how big you want them to be in your quilt. Some panels have no obvious space between the images, and the panel itself might not be square. In this instance, cut your image on the obvious lines, which might be indicated by color or a printed border or line. Once they are cut apart, square up each image.

To square up a panel image, select any logical line of the image—I generally choose the top.

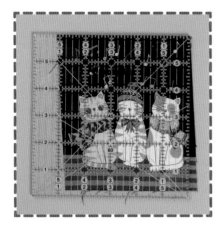  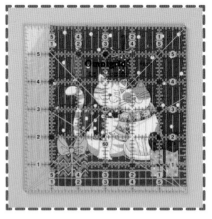

1. Align a ruler edge along that line to determine how **not** square the piece is. This will show you which sides or corners you'll need to manipulate to straighten the image.

2. With a spray bottle of water, lightly mist the fabric. Iron the corner or section of the image until it is as square as possible. Work slowly and check the shape regularly.

3. Spritz, press, check with the ruler, and repeat until the image is as straight as you can manage.

4. Finally, spray it lightly with starch, place something flat (such as a large ruler) over the piece, and stack some books on top until it has dried into the shape you want to achieve.

MEASURING PANEL IMAGES

I begin by measuring and understanding the **finished size** of the panel images. This detail is important because these panels will be inserted in the open spaces within the blocks themselves or in the open spaces that are inherently created by repeating blocks.

For example, here is a portion of a panel I used for the *Santa Paws Is Coming to Town* row-by-row quilt (page 50). The panel images measure 5˝ × 5 ¾˝ inches when cut apart.

Depending on the size I need for the blocks I am working on, now would be the time to trim them down to a usable size or to add some coping strips to bring the panel image **up** to a size that will work. I actually used both of these techniques for this quilt.

ADDING COPING STRIPS

Coping strips are useful when a panel segment is too small for the space allowed. To bring it up to the size needed, you may have to add strips to some, or all of the edges of the image. Coping strips are not the same as a border because they serve the purpose of getting you from the size you have to the size you need.

Square Up First

Before you do anything to the panel images—trimming them or adding coping strips—be sure to square them up!

For example, let's say your panel image finishes at 4½˝, but it needs to finish at 6˝ to fit the space in the design. It is important to always remember to graph in **finished** sizes!

Knowing that your image has to be 6˝, determine the difference between where you're going (6˝) and where you are (4½˝). The difference is 1½˝. I prefer to keep the coping strips the same size whenever possible, but it's not a requirement. What is important is that the math works!

Divide 1½˝ by 2 to make the strips the same size on each edge. This equals ¾˝ for each edge. *Stop* and remember that you are graphing in *finished* sizes. Cut the strips 1¼˝ wide to include the ¼˝ seam allowance on both sides.

Let's walk through this process in detail:

1. The panel image finishes at 4½˝ × 4½˝, so it is cut at 5˝ × 5˝ to include seam allowances.

2. Cut the strips as follows: 2 strips 1¼˝ × 5˝ and 2 strips 1¼˝ × 6½˝. This accounts for the width you have now added to the sides of the image.

3. Add the shorter strips to the sides first, and then the longer strips to the top and bottom. The panel piece should now measure 6½˝ × 6½˝, which will finish at 6˝ × 6˝.

DETERMINING THE GRID

Most quilt blocks are built on a grid, so a basic understanding of and the ability to recognize the grid that a quilt block is based on are essential. Simply put, understand that the block can be divided equally across (rows) and up and down (columns).

The most common and familiar grids are 3 × 3 and 2 × 2 (sometimes referred to as 4 × 4). The simplest example of a 3 × 3 grid is a Nine Patch block, and the most basic 2 × 2 is a Four Patch block. I often subdivide a 2 × 2 grid into a 4 × 4 because it helps me identify the individual units that make up more complex or detailed blocks.

Some blocks, such as a 6˝ block, could be used in a 3 × 3 or a 4 × 4 grid. The grid changes the size of the units, but the basic block remains 6˝.

The grid is important because your panel image may fit in a 3 × 3 grid, but not in a 4 × 4, and vice versa. Selecting complementary blocks based on size may also be determined by grids, as you might have a space for a traditional block that may not fit if the grid is not compatible.

For example, take a look at the Sawtooth Star block in the top row of the *Santa Paws Is Coming to Town* quilt (page 50). The Sawtooth Star block is based on a 4 × 4 grid. The panel image was not compatible with a 4 × 4 grid because of the size. To use it in the center of this block, I had to add coping strips.

Remember to graph in **finished** sizes and to ensure that the block divides into a grid size you are comfortable working with. A 6˝ block divided into a 3 × 3 grid results in 2˝ units. A 6˝ block divided into a 4 × 4 grid results in 1½˝ units.

Try to avoid working with ⅛˝ or ¼˝ measurements. The beautiful point in all of this instruction is that the blocks and the quilt can be whatever size is going to work for you, so keep the math simple and make it easy on yourself!

Let's look at each of the styles of quilts we've discussed so far and talk about how to make the math work.

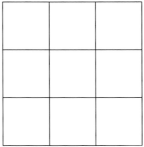
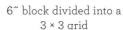

6˝ block divided into a
3 × 3 grid

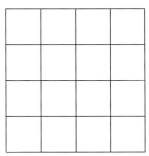

6˝ block divided into a
4 × 4 grid

REPEATED BLOCK SETTING QUILTS

When working with a repeated block setting, such as the Irish Chain quilt (page 13), begin with the finished size of the panel images. Because you are repeating a specific block in a predetermined size, your panel images must all be the same size. Before proceeding, decide whether:

• It will be easiest to make the math work by using the panel image as is.

• You'll need to add a coping strip around each panel image to make it larger.

• You should trim each panel image slightly to make it smaller.

This is a **big** decision, so don't rush it. You will want that panel image to be a size that makes the rest of the pattern easy to work with.

Using panel pieces in a one- or two-block quilt requires only that the panel pieces and the corresponding pattern work mathematically. The number of blocks and rows depends on how many panel images you have and whether you are going to intersperse the blocks featuring panel images with

blocks that don't have images to make the quilt a specific size.

You will want to do a little preplanning and begin this style of quilt knowing how big you want it to be when it is finished. If you don't have enough panel images to construct the number of blocks you need for the rows, then you have several options:

• Use several of the same or a complementary panel with same-size images so you can make more blocks.

• Change the size of the quilt.

• Alternate with a different block that doesn't feature panel images.

• Change the size of the panel images within the blocks by adding coping strips (page 27).

• Add sashing between the blocks and rows.

• Place the blocks on point.

All of these options will increase the size of a quilt. If you want a smaller quilt, simply use fewer panel images and fewer blocks.

Once you've followed all the steps to square up the panel images; added coping strips, if needed; decided how many blocks to make, depending on the finished size of the quilt; and confirmed that all the math is correct, it's time to start cutting, sewing, and finishing. Have fun!

Graph in Finished Sizes

Remember to work with **finished sizes** as you do these calculations and to add the seam allowance when cutting!

Let's use my *Dr. Seuss Goes to Ireland* quilt (page 15) to walk through the steps of graphing a repeat block quilt:

1. Measure the panel images to decide the finished size. The Dr. Seuss's ABC panel had 5⅛˝ images, measuring only the colored portion of the images. They were easily trimmed to 5˝ without losing any of the design, for a finished size of 4½˝.

2. Determine the grid upon which the surrounding block is based. I used an Irish Chain pattern, which is based on a Nine Patch block with a 3 × 3 grid.

3. Once you know the grid, ask yourself whether the finished size of your panel image divides equally into

a measurement you can easily use within that grid format. My Dr. Seuss panel images would **finish** at 4½˝.

Does 4½˝ divide equally and comfortably into a 3 × 3 grid? **Yes**, 4½˝ divided by 3 means that each square within the 3 × 3 grid would finish at 1½˝. This gave me Nine Patch blocks made up of 1½˝ squares. The block and panel image sizes worked out mathematically. I added sashing and cornerstones to frame the letters and make the quilt larger.

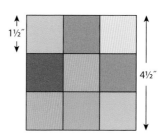 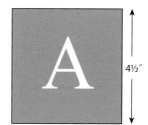

Some patterns are easier than others to manipulate in this manner. For example, a Log Cabin quilt can be made of blocks using any strip size you want. Additionally, the center (where you would highlight your panel image) can also be any size you want, making this design a really easy and simple quilt block to get your toes wet with.

Log Cabin Exercise

Suppose that your panel pieces will finish at 5˝ × 5˝. You want to make a quilt using 9˝ blocks. Determine the dimensions of your strips. Keep it simple—this question has several solutions. See Exercise Solutions (page 48).

Sister's Choice Exercise

Next, let's work with a variation of the Sister's Choice block. You can see the finished quilt in the Gallery, *Baby's Besties* (page 56). This block is based on a 4 × 4 grid, and the center uses 2 sections across and 2 sections up and down withing the grid (a 2 × 2 grid).

To determine whether your panel pieces will work in this block, measure the images. Decide whether the size will divide equally into a 2 × 2 grid or whether you'll need to add coping strips to fit the center of the block.

If your panel image finishes at 6˝ × 6˝, graph the block so that a 6˝ panel image will fit in the block center without having to add coping strips. To check whether you got it right, refer to Exercise Solutions (page 48).

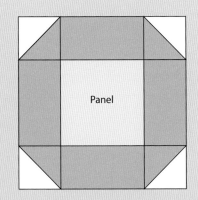

Panel

ROW-BY-ROW QUILTS

Perhaps the most important thing to keep in mind with a row-by-row quilt is that all the rows **must** be the same width for the quilt to work. Although that concept seems simple and logical, making the elements within the rows fit that measurement can be a little more challenging.

I begin my row-by-row quilts in pretty much the same manner I begin all of my panel quilts: I measure the panel images after squaring them up. You'll need to know what kind of flexibility you have to use the images within traditional quilt blocks or as repeated elements in your design. For a refresher, see Measuring Panel Images (page 26).

When creating a row-by-row quilt, I use a graph paper map to ensure that everything fits together. If you've mastered a computer program for designing, of course, that works too! To see how this process comes together, let's take a look at my *Love and a Dog* row-by-row quilt (page 10).

Using the suggestions in Finding Design Features (page 18), I determined that I wanted rows with the themes of hearts, pawprints, doghouses, bones, fire hydrants, and framed panel images. Some of the quotes within the panel also guided me to specific quilt blocks I selected to highlight different images, such as the King's Crown block variation. Here is how I made it all work:

1. I determined that I had 16 panel images to work with. I chose to create four rows that included four panel images in each row. I highlighted the actual panel images within traditional and not-so-traditional quilt blocks, such as doghouses, the King's Crown block variation, Framed Squares, and the ever-important fire hydrant.

2. Then, I focused on themed rows that fit my subject matter, such as hearts, paw prints, and dog bones, to alternate with the panel image rows. I included themed rows because row-by-row quilts usually have a variety of motifs that relate to one another. The themed rows make the quilt interesting and provide visual appeal. Having a variety of row heights also keeps the viewer involved and draws their eye around the quilt. Another benefit to adding themed rows is to increase the quilt's top-to-bottom length.

Don't hesitate to mix up the techniques you use! Combine appliqué designs, pieced blocks, foundation-pieced blocks, embroidered blocks, and so forth. Mixing up the techniques adds more interest.

Using a Grid on Your Design Wall

Using grid flannel on your design wall helps you visually get a feel for the size of your rows as well as how much area to fill creatively between blocks.

3. Next, I started with the panel images that would be featured within traditional quilt blocks or that I wanted to group together in a single row. For my *Love and a Dog* quilt (page 10), I began with the doghouses and graphed a block that would feature the 6″ × 6″ panel images in a nice-sized doghouse block that finished at 12″ × 12″. Four of these blocks gave me a row width of 48″. You'll need to graph one or more of your blocks at this stage to begin working out the math. For guidance on creating your own traditionally pieced blocks, see Graphing Unique Traditionally Pieced Blocks (page 38).

4. Then, I played with the King's Crown variation to see what size block I could use to come close to the same measurement. Remember, not all of your blocks have to be the same size; the rows have to end up the same width, but varying the sizes of the blocks offers you options for creative fill.

Don't sweat the small stuff! If the blocks aren't going to come out the same size, don't abandon them—instead, think creatively and find a way to fill the leftover space with something appealing (avoid plain strips of fabric if you can!). Interesting options could include checkerboards, half-square triangles, flying geese, pinwheels, small quilt blocks, and much more—let your imagination take you where it will. As long as all the math works out in the end, your choice of filler is what will capture the interest of the viewer and enhance the design of the quilt.

EMBROIDERED BLOCKS

Embroidered blocks can add a lot of interest to your quilts. The embroidery sits on top of the quilt, so in addition to offering visual interest, these blocks provide texture.

There are so many sources for embroidered motifs! Traditional and machine embroidery motifs are easy to find with a simple Internet search. You can also find several embroidery books listed in the Resources (page 62).

As with any block you add, the most important tip is to be sure that the block sizes add up to the correct width for the rows.

My design for the King's Crown block finished at 9″ × 9″. Four blocks in a row equaled 36″, but my rows needed to be 48″ wide. I was left with 12″ to fill with something interesting.

Because the outside edges of the blocks were busy, I chose to separate the blocks with three sections, each 4″ wide. I decided that checkerboards would be perfect, so I made a 2″-wide checkerboard strip using 1″ squares with a 1″ solid strip on either side to make the checkerboards "float".

Don't Stress

The blocks don't all have to be the same size! Variety is the spice of life and the visual spice of a Row quilt!

5. I followed this same process for the framed squares. Using this block offered me some options—I could have made the frames larger because nothing was keeping me from using wider strips and bigger squares—but I didn't want the frame to overwhelm the panel image. I settled on a smaller size and opted to separate the blocks with some flying geese units. Once again, use your imagination and try to avoid inserting plain strips of fabric; I know you're more creative than that!

6. The fire hydrants were easy to graph to the same size as the doghouses, 12˝ × 12˝. I found a picture of a fire hydrant online and graphed my block from there.

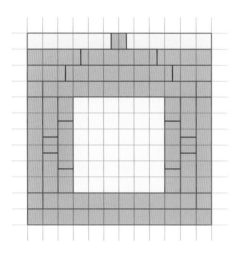

7. When working out my themed rows, I tend to keep them smaller than the block rows that feature the panel images. There is no set rule here—just select a size that looks appealing between the rows. I usually keep these between 3˝ and 5˝, but remember, it's your quilt, so you get to make those decisions!

I plan my appliqué designs so that they almost fill the background strip, and I space them visually. The hearts and pawprints were done in this manner. I don't measure—I like a more organic approach—but if measuring makes you more comfortable, by all means, space your appliqué motifs with a ruler!

When working with a pieced element, such as the dog bone blocks, I make sure that the width of the row matches the width of all the other rows. My dog bone blocks were 4˝ × 4˝, and because 4 divides evenly into 48, the math told me that I needed to construct 12 blocks.

Once again, this point is where the math comes in handy—you may have to adjust the size of the pieced elements to match the width of your row or include spacers between elements. It's always about the math! But knowing that the math is going to work out is a rewarding part of the process. Here's my final map for this project.

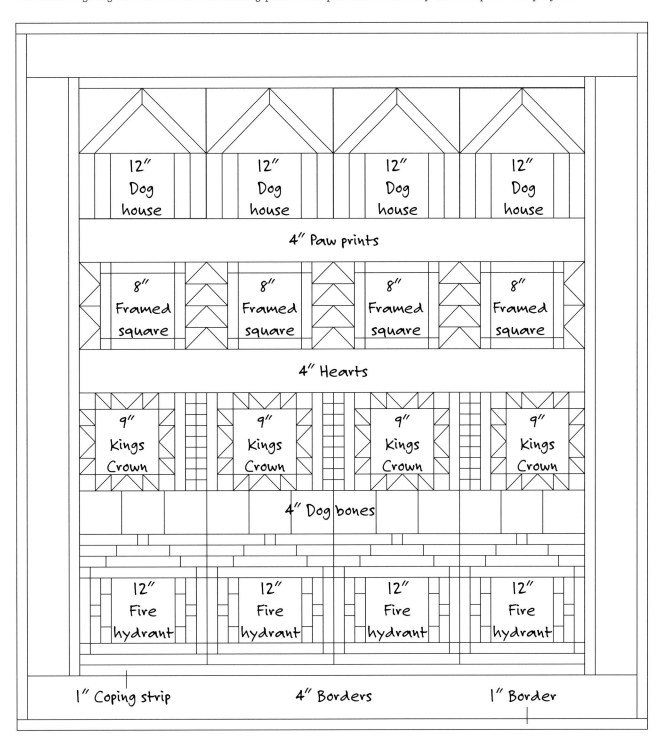

To see how some of my students and I creatively dealt with making all of our rows work together, take a look at some of the other row-by-row quilts in the Gallery (page 49).

MONTAGE QUILTS

The math of the montage is perhaps the most complex and most reliant on your graphed grid or map. Without this tool, the chances of making this quilt come together are greatly diminished. There's also the probability that you might figuratively paint yourself into a corner. But don't let that possibility scare you—making a map is much easier than you might think!

The final size of your montage will reveal itself as you put everything on your graph paper. Once you start committing to the location of the panel pieces and all the other elements you plan to include, the finished size of your quilt will become more evident. Of course, you may wish to add interesting borders, which can also affect the finished size.

Montage quilts require a different approach as you refine your ideas on graph paper. A couple of ideas for approaching the design map include using a gridded felt design wall, card stock, or a printout of your panel on graph paper.

Gridded Design Wall

Consider beginning the plan for your montage on a gridded flannel design wall. Placing your panel pieces onto a grid can help you begin to get a strong visual sense of how the piece might come together. Because we quilters tend to be very visual, I love having the grid behind my pieces as I move them around.

Some of the most fun, and some of the biggest challenges, I have had in the past couple of years has come from designing a montage! Start by scattering your prepared panel images around the design wall to get a feel for where they will live when the project is completed. Your gridded design wall will also help you plan the open spaces where you'll insert words and creative fill.

Do you have images and elements spaced too far apart or too close together? Do you need to add a spacer or a place for some of your words? Is the quilt drawing your eye around to the different elements, or is it causing you to stop somewhere? Do you like the flow? Can you see someplace that could use a different kind or size of fill?

After you have played with the arrangement of the images, transfer the basics of the design to graph paper. This map will help you refine and finalize the design and work out the math involved.

Planning with Printouts

If you do not have a gridded design wall, try this approach. Find a photo of the panel online and, with a little fussing, print it so that the panel images come out to a size that actually works with your graph paper. For example, an 8″ × 8″ panel image reduced and printed at 1″ could be used on your graph paper representing 2 squares to the inch.

If you can't find the image or can't adjust it to print to scale, try substituting construction paper or card stock to represent the panel image. Cut the paper to match the scale of your design. Label the pieces so you know which is which because the panel images likely do have placements that are more pleasing or logical. For example, you probably don't want that sailboat to end up over the sun! Once you have them cut and labeled, you can then move them around on your graph paper until you find a layout that is pleasing to the eye, much like designing a room with cutouts of furniture.

Finishing the Quilt Map

After you have the panel images finalized on your grid, you can get creative in filling in all the spaces around them. The graph paper map will help you know the sizes of the spaces you need to fill.

Regardless of whether you used a design wall or started with graph paper, you have to decide what goes into those empty spaces. Get your ideas down on scratch paper before committing everything to graph paper. Try loosely sketching your layout onto plain paper and start to doodle—yes, doodle—what you might fill in around the panel pieces. Look back on the brainstorming exercises and the notes you made while studying the panel before actually beginning the project. Look for themes and ideas that may lead to traditional quilt blocks, appliqué motifs, and any words to use in the piece.

Sometimes, those ideas come fairly quickly, but at other times, it takes a bit more effort. What you choose to fill in the empty spaces should reflect the theme of your montage as well as the images that are already present in your panel.

Be creative, have fun, and don't just insert plain chunks of fabric if you can put something whimsical in a space. And remember to check, double check, and triple check your measurements and your math along the way.

Beach Day 48˝ × 52˝ Montage quilt by the author

Let's take a look at the map for my *Beach Day* quilt to see what I mean. Once I had the panel pieces set, I began to sketch in blocks that complemented the panel images. Getting it all on graph paper was key to ensuring that it would all fit successfully.

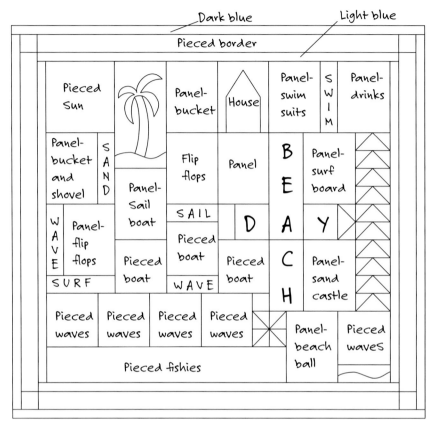

You can see that I added a sun (there were several in the panel), a palm tree, a bathhouse, flip-flops, sailboats, waves, a school of fish, and some smaller filler in a few other spots.

The sun reminded me of a Dresden Plate block, so I used a quarter of a Dresden Plate block to create the sun in the upper left corner. The palm tree and the flip-flops were actually in one of the panel images, so for these, I used the panel itself to create patterns for the appliquéd blocks. See Creating Appliqué Motifs (page 46).

I graphed my own sailboat block to fit the size I had calculated for pieced boats and graphed my own bathhouse as well. I likely could have found patterns for these elements, but honestly, it was faster just to graph my own! To graph your own pieced blocks, see Graphing Unique Traditionally Pieced Blocks (page 38).

I had seen photos of the Snail's Trail block constructed in all watercolors, so that was an easy choice. The fish took a little bit of imagination, and this is where I embellished with the wiggly eyes!

My montage quilts all feature appliqué words. I like to add one section of words as a "title" for them. I make this section larger, with larger letters, so that I draw the attention of the viewer to these words first. Notice on the various montage quilts throughout the book that most have one set of words that convey the title of the piece. The title section gives the viewer an idea of what you want them to see. Remember that the font you select also evokes a feeling, so choose carefully. To learn how to create your own text blocks, check out Creating Text as Appliqué (page 47).

In some of the smaller spots, I added some traditional patchwork blocks. Lastly, I added a column of flying geese along one side of the quilt, parallel to the title, to reflect the sunrise.

Making a Construction Plan

Okay, now you've got your quilt map, but there's one more step! You need to create a construction plan from the gridded map in order to sew your creation together. In reality, sewing a montage quilt is not quite the same as piecing a quilt in rows. Look for and mark the pieces that can be sewn together in sections or chunks.

Here is my construction plan for my *Beach Day* quilt. You can see how I pieced together columns and then joined the columns into sections. In the end, I did have to sew one partial seam to join it all together. Although I really try hard to avoid those, sometimes they happen. Just do your best to keep them to a minimum so you don't drive yourself crazy!

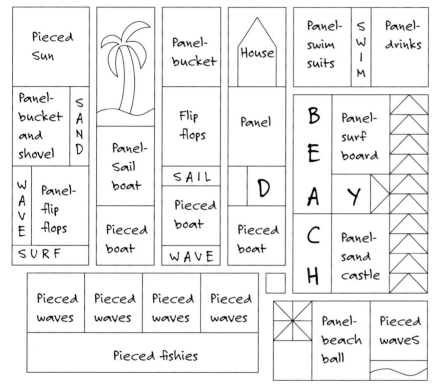

Before we finish our discussion of row-by-row and montage quilts, let's take a look at borders. These styles of quilts have a **lot** of creativity poured into them, so to add plain, slab borders in the end seems almost criminal. You could use a repeated shape that is prominent in the quilt, add appliqué motifs, or even feature text in the border of a montage quilt. You might have to dig deep to find some inspiration to do a pieced or appliquéd border, but I think you'll agree that even something as simple as added interest in two of the corners is better than a plain slab of fabric. Don't scrimp on the borders!

Many times, we quilters finish the body of a piece and seem to run out of ideas. Instead of taking a little more time to create an interesting border, we simply sew on a few basic borders and call the project finished. If you can add something that will finish the piece with a flourish, I encourage you to do so! And finally, before stressing about borders, ask yourself whether the piece even *needs* borders! A wonderful example of a quilt that needed no borders is *The 19th Hole* montage quilt by Terry Helmer (page 11).

GRAPHING UNIQUE TRADITIONALLY PIECED BLOCKS

By now, you should be able tell that I am encouraging you to **be creative**, design your own quilt, and stretch yourself! Row-by-row and montage quilts allow you, as a creative quilter, to step outside your comfort zone and begin to draw your own quilt blocks. In my workshops, I encourage my students to take off their floaties and jump into the deep end with me—no more wading in the kiddie pool!

At first, graphing your own blocks might seem intimidating, but dear quilter, if you want a cowboy boot block and no one in the quilting world has created a cowboy boot that you like, then your choices are to forget that fabulous idea or figure it out for yourself. I vote for figuring it out. You can do this!

Here are a few important points to keep in mind, just in case you haven't done any graphing:

• Always work in finished sizes.

• Define the outer perimeter of the block first.

• Identify shapes/units that compose the full block.

GRAPHING EXERCISES FOR SIMPLE BLOCKS

I needed a Barn block to fit a specific space in my *She Sheds* montage quilt (page 49). My daughter's she shed is her barn, so as a tribute to her, I just had to include a barn. I couldn't find a barn block I liked so—you guessed it—I had to figure out how to create my own.

I began by looking at lots of pictures of barns—but keep it simple, sweetheart (KISS)! You don't need a complex design, just enough to provide the viewer with the basic idea.

Here are several barn images that I used as a jumping-off point.

I liked the last one in the third row best and decided that I could graph something similar with just a few shapes.

Next, I divided the drawing into a number of workable shapes I am familiar with in the world of quilting. These shapes became the units that made up the quilt block. I outlined squares, rectangles, and half-square triangles— and that was it! Don't forget that the background is composed of shapes, too, and also needs to be graphed.

Additionally, try to keep such shapes as half-square triangles or flying geese in measurements you are comfortable working with. It's your block, so you can adjust the size of the individual units or pieces as needed to accommodate the space and the size that is going to be most workable. It's easier to work with a 2″ half-square triangle than it is to work with a 2¼″ half-square triangle. If you need to adjust the size of your block to fit the space, the background is probably the easiest place to figure out the tricky math and the place that offers the most flexibility.

Once I have shapes that can be pieced together, I move to graph paper. I had already determined the necessary block dimensions, so I outlined them onto my graph paper, as illustrated.

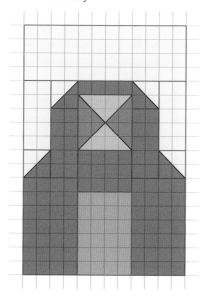

Once they were graphed, I adjusted some of the shapes a little bit for ease of construction or to fit my defined space more easily. And just for fun, in this quilt and on this barn, I decided to replace the square door at the top with a pieced block representing a barn quilt!

You will need to analyze the drawn blocks to be sure that you can piece them easily and efficiently. You should draw your block on graph paper because this will illustrate what shapes make up the block. Once you have the graph lines behind the image, you will start to identify shapes, such as squares, rectangles, half-square triangles, and so forth. Keep the units that you identify as simple as possible.

If you are a seasoned quilter, the shapes in the barn block should jump out at you. Beginners may find this idea a little tricky at first, but careful study of the block will reveal the shapes mentioned above. If you find something that seems especially intricate or confusing to piece together, redraw the block to be constructed of basic shapes, such as squares, rectangles, and triangles. Whenever possible, you'll want to avoid Y-seams or anything that turns a corner.

Keep Your Finished Design in Mind

Remember that for a row-by-row quilt, all that has to happen is that when all the blocks come together, the row must be the same width as all the other rows. If you're doing a single block for a montage quilt, then simply adjust the block or the surrounding areas to accommodate a measurement that works best for your design.

Bell Exercise

This little Christmas bell is a fun project to graph on your own. Try graphing this motif onto a 6″ quilt block. Play around with the shape of the bow and make the bell your own! Check out possible solutions at the end of this chapter, under Bell Solutions (page 48).

CUTTING THE PIECES

I can't emphasize enough that graphing happens in **finished** sizes. All seam allowances need to be added to the individual shapes or units that you have drawn. For example, if your graphed block has squares that will finish at 2″, be sure to cut them out at 2½″. **Always add your seam allowance before you cut.**

BLOCK CONSTRUCTION

Another consideration is the actual construction of your block. When creating pieced designs, be sure that you are working with straight lines when dividing the block for construction purposes. Nobody likes Y-seams, so, like potholes, if you can avoid them, do!

Take the time to discover how each block you draw can most easily be pieced together. Work from the smallest units, such as half-square triangles, to rows, to finally piecing the larger sections together.

Let's look at the barn illustrated earlier.

After I identify all the shapes in the block, I identify which shapes should be put together first: the *piecing order.* Think back to the first quilt blocks you made. Most beginner blocks are pieced together in a simple and logical fashion. A Nine Patch block is constructed of 3 rows of 3 squares each. A Rail Fence block is created by sewing 3 or 4 strips together. More complex blocks basically follow this same construction technique.

The barn block is constructed in columns, each containing triangles and squares and/or rectangles. Once each column is constructed, they are joined, and the top section is added. Piece beginning with the smallest units and moving to the larger sections.

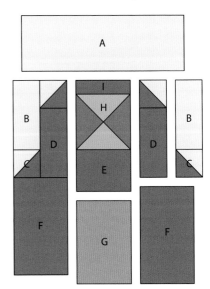

Let's look at another example. In my row-by-row quilt *Santa Paws Is Coming to Town* (page 50), I wanted to create a row of ugly Christmas sweaters. I didn't have a resource for a pieced sweater, so I searched online for line drawings of sweaters and found this one.

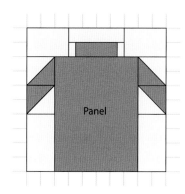

I simplified the shape for my 10˝ block. The body of the sweater is a large rectangle, the turtle neck is a smaller rectangle, and each sleeve is made of half-square triangles. I decided where the panel images were going to go, added a row of random patchwork to enhance the "ugly" design of the sweater, and .. success!

To piece this block together, first identify the block components. If you choose to do something fun with the sweater body, do that first. The **finished** size pieces are as follows:

Piece A, sweater body, 1 rectangle 6˝ × 8˝

Piece B, sleeves, 4 half-square triangles 2˝ × 2˝

Piece C, background, 2 rectangles 2˝ × 4˝

Piece D, background, 2 rectangles 2˝ × 3˝

Piece E, collar, 1 rectangle 1˝ × 3˝

Piece F, background, 2 rectangles ½˝ × 1˝

Piece G, background, 1 rectangle 1˝ × 4˝

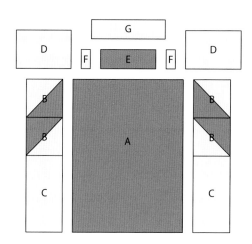

My ugly sweater block was pieced in a slightly different order than my barn block.

The piecing order is as follows:

1. Make 4 half-square triangle B units. Sew together in pairs for the sleeves.

2. Add a background piece C to each sleeve.

3. Sew the sleeve units to the sides of sweater body piece A. Set aside.

4. Sew a background piece F to the sides of collar piece E.

5. Add background piece G to the top and background pieces D to the sides of the collar unit. Sew to the top of the set-aside sweater body section.

Paper or foundation piecing can be the perfect solution to creating a design that just won't work in a grid. Some blocks are better and more easily pieced on a foundation, and this method could be the answer to creating a design that is a little more free-form. The trees are paper-pieced blocks I drew for my *Sunflower Pastures* montage quilt (page 22).

There are many different methods of doing this kind of piecing. Most require a foundation, such as paper, stabilizer, vellum, fabric, or even freezer paper. The design is mirrored and then printed or traced onto the chosen foundation. The fabric is sewn onto the back of the foundation with a very small stitch, which will aid in the removal of the foundation after the block is completed.

Use a Larger Needle

You may also consider using a larger needle, such as size 90/14, for foundation piecing. This larger needle will create larger holes in the foundation, which can aid in the removal of the foundation material.

To begin drawing your pattern, first determine the finished block dimensions, and then add the details of the design within that boundary. Be sure that some of the design lines touch the boundary—the design cannot float in space. It has to connect to, or anchor to, an edge of the block.

Try to have the fewest number of units possible. Keep lines and units as simple and clean as possible. No Y-seams—everything you draw should be a straight

seam to sew. The more lines you make, the more detailed and complex your block will be.

I suggest moving seam lines and deleting smaller details until you have the smallest number of lines possible that still convey the essence of the shape. You don't need to include all the details; simple and straightforward lines that convey the essence of the design are all that are needed.

Next, break up each section into the smaller pieces that make up the design by color. These section lines will follow the large shapes in the drawing. **All lines should connect between any two lines already in place.**

Some quilt block patterns can be foundation-pieced all in one section, which means that you can start with one piece of fabric in the middle or on one end and then add pieces in sequence to cover the whole foundation. Others must be pieced in sections, with the sections then joined. As you draw your paper-pieced pattern, you will determine to which of these categories your block belongs.

A Square in a Square is a simple block that could be foundation-pieced. The piecing sequence is noted by the numbers; you add the pieces in order. Starting with piece 1 and ending with piece 9, this block can be pieced all in one section.

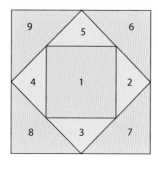

The Five-Pointed Star block falls into the second category: blocks that are more intricate and need to be broken down into separate sections.

Let's look at a simple Five-Pointed Star block. First, define the boundary and then draw the star within that space. Draw the lines so that the major lines of the

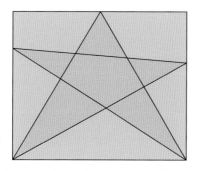

design actually touch the outer boundary at several points.

Divide your drawing into major sections; this could be just two sections but might be more, depending on the design. Make these lines heavy and dark—these are the last seams sewn, and

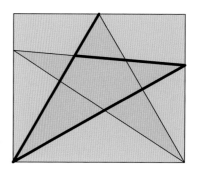

every complex block has one or more. These lines might be horizontal, vertical, or diagonal. These heavier lines will also help you understand where to define the individual units that make up the whole.

Each of the major sections of this paper-pieced block is colored differently in the illustration to the right. This is to show that each is a stand-alone section that has

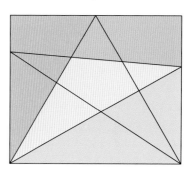

to be pieced independently before the sections are sewn together to create this star block.

If you create a pattern with multiple sections, you may wish to label each foundation with a letter to illustrate the individual sections that will be

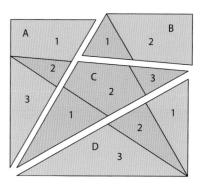

joined together. In this example, there are actually four sections: A, B, C, and D.

Determine a workable order for piecing and number them so that nothing is overlapping and the number order is logical and clean. There is no **one** right way to do this, but in general, if a section joins to a seamed piece, then the seamed section must be constructed first.

Any line that has seams protruding from both sides will be a split in the foundation and, therefore, create a separate foundation unit. Next, decide on the order in which to piece each foundation, remembering that if a section joins to a seamed piece, then the seamed section must be numbered first.

Separate the individual sections and be sure to add ¼˝ seam allowance to each section so that as you sew them together, the piecing works out perfectly.

Test the pattern and adjust as needed.

Foundations Piece in Reverse

As a reminder, foundation-pieced patterns will finish in the reverse of what is drawn. If you want the pattern to be oriented in a specific direction, you will need to trace it on the other side of your original and create your foundations from this reversed pattern.

Lighthouse Exercise

Just as you can draw your own patterns for traditionally pieced blocks from pictures or images, you can create patterns for paper-pieced blocks. Adapt this image of a lighthouse for a paper-pieced version. Start by tracing the outline onto tracing paper and then simplify the lines by erasing unnecessary details. Remember, you're just trying to get a simple shape or series of shapes that will cause the viewer to see a lighthouse. Don't include details that might make the piecing too complex or too detailed.

In this drawing, I would delete most of the details, such as the waves at the base and the light rays on the tower. Keep the shapes simple and clean. After you have drawn your pattern, determine your piecing order and decide whether the block will need to be pieced in sections. See how I drew this pattern in Exercise Solutions (page 48).

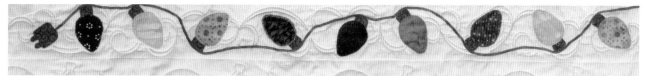

CREATING YOUR OWN
APPLIQUÉ PATTERNS

Appliqué is a great option when you want to include a shape that cannot be easily pieced by using traditional methods. Examples included rounded heart shapes, flip-flops, bows, flowers, and so forth.

Holiday lights, complete with plug. Detail of *Santa Paws Is Coming to Town* (page 50)

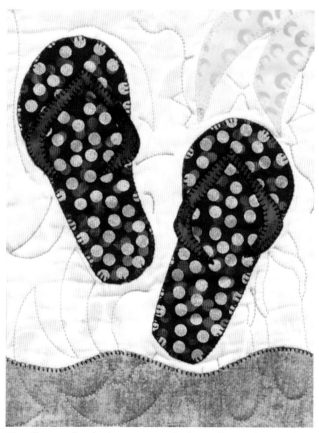

Flip-flops and palm leaves. Detail of *Beach Day* (page 35)

The following sections discuss techniques for creating appliqué shapes and appliqué words for your montage quilts.

CREATING APPLIQUÉ MOTIFS

If you're new to appliqué, many great resources provide step-by-step instructions on how to do needle-turn appliqué, raw-edge appliqué, and other appliqué techniques. For suggestions, see Resources (page 62).

You can find appliqué motifs in any number of places. You may be able to find the one you want commercially available and ready to go. If you are able, consider drawing your own motifs. You can also explore other resources for appliqué patterns, such as coloring books, the Internet, children's drawings, greeting cards, or even the panel you are featuring in your quilt—the sky's the limit!

On my *Love and a Dog* quilt (page 10), I added a row of hearts. One of the panel images includes a heart. Had I wished to use that exact heart in my filler row, I could have taken my panel image to my home printer/copier and photocopied it. Next, I could have used it as is or enlarged it to the desired size and then used it as an appliqué pattern. Any motif within your panel can provide you with a ready-made appliqué pattern—simply photocopy the fabric and enlarge or reduce it to the desired size!

Keep Copyright in Mind!

Keep in mind that when you photocopy a motif from anywhere, including your panel, it is for your personal use only. Please respect copyright! Selling or marketing a design as an appliqué pattern of your own is in violation of copyright laws.

You can enlarge or reduce your chosen image to a size that will work for you and your project. For some motifs, you may wish to reverse the image if you want it to face the same direction as in your panel. Remember that in general, designs for machine appliqué are drawn or fused onto the back side of the fabric, so the image will be reversed when it is completed.

In other words, if you have a palm tree that is leaning to the right, reverse your photocopied image. Then, when the tree is printed or traced onto the fusible, which is going onto the back of the fabric, the palm tree will also be leaning to the right once the appliqué is completed.

Fusible Products

Some fusible products can be printed with your home printer! This saves time and makes this step faster and easier—be sure to print a test on paper first to ensure that you like the size. Often, you end up needing images, words, or letters to be much bigger than you might imagine.

If you have motifs or elements of your panel that you're not incorporating elsewhere, consider cutting them out and using them as an appliqué motif within a traditional block or elsewhere on the quilt. I do this for row-by-row and montage quilts. Highlighting an image from the panel creates another layer of whimsy and focus.

CREATING TEXT AS APPLIQUÉ

Creating templates for appliqué words to use in montage quilts is a simple matter of some familiarity with your word-processing program. Test different fonts to find the one you believe fits the style of your quilt. Also test different font sizes for the space on the quilt. I leave a space or two between letters unless the font is cursive writing.

I follow these steps in Microsoft Word for creating my templates:

1. Insert a text box into a document by clicking *Insert > Text Box*, and then type and format your text.

2. Right-click the box and click *Format Shape*.

3. In the *Format Shape* pane, click *Effects*.

4. Highlight the text and then click on the pentagon-shaped option to reverse your text.

5. Print your reversed text directly onto fusible web sheets (inkjet printers only). Fuse to the fabric, and you're ready to go!

Note: Your word-processing program may have this option in a slightly different set of steps, such as having to click on *3-D Rotation > X-Rotation > 180°*. You can search the Help menu or search the Internet for how to reverse text in your program.

Here's an example:

Insert the text box.

Type and format your text.

In the *Format Shape* pane, click *Effects*.

Highlight the text and then click on the pentagon symbol to instantly reverse your text.

Now, you can print your reversed text directly onto fusible, fuse to fabric, and *go*!

EXERCISE SOLUTIONS

LOG CABIN SOLUTION

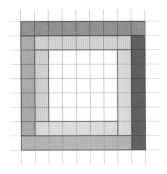

SISTER'S CHOICE
VARIATION SOLUTION

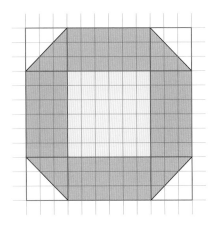

LIGHTHOUSE SOLUTION

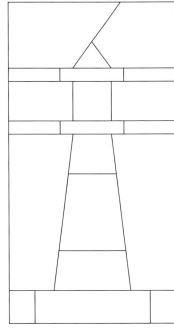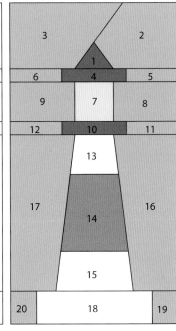

BELL SOLUTIONS

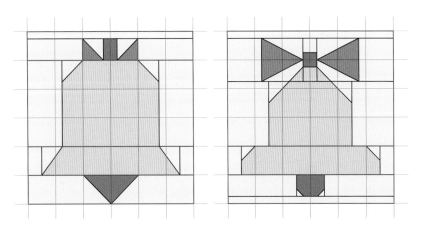

She Sheds 51˝ × 41˝ Montage quilt by the author (cover quilt)
Folkscapes panel by Karla Gerard for Benartex Designer Fabrics

I spent several weeks exploring ideas for the panel I used in this quilt, and one day I walked into my studio and the panel jumped out and shouted—*she sheds*! I had a lot of fun embellishing this one, including adding buttons, bells, pins, and even a free-hanging mini-quilt!

Santa Paws Is Coming to Town 70˝ × 70˝ Row-by-row quilt by the author
Santa Paws panel by Makower UK

In this row-by-row quilt, I was experimenting with "shadow" blocks. I used the same blocks in the rows but kept some grayed out so that I could create the illusion of a Christmas tree with the colored blocks in each row.

Susan Scissorhand 40˝ × 37½˝ Montage quilt by Susan Wiley
A Ghastlie Craft panel by Alexander Henry Fabrics

Susan recalls, "I had so much fun just letting my imagination go, but at the same time keeping within the parameters Cyndi gave in the class. I loved all her suggestions for what to possibly incorporate. I used words, spool blocks, three little traditional quilt blocks, appliqués, and embellished with a variety of buttons (cats, spools, scissors) while keeping it all just a little bit wonky like the featured ladies."

Circle of Friends 80˝ × 90˝ Repeated block quilt by the author
Jungle Friends panel by Jason Yenter for In the Beginning Fabrics

I love the big open space created when this setting of Friendship Stars is configured. It created a perfect space in which to highlight the jungle friends of this panel.

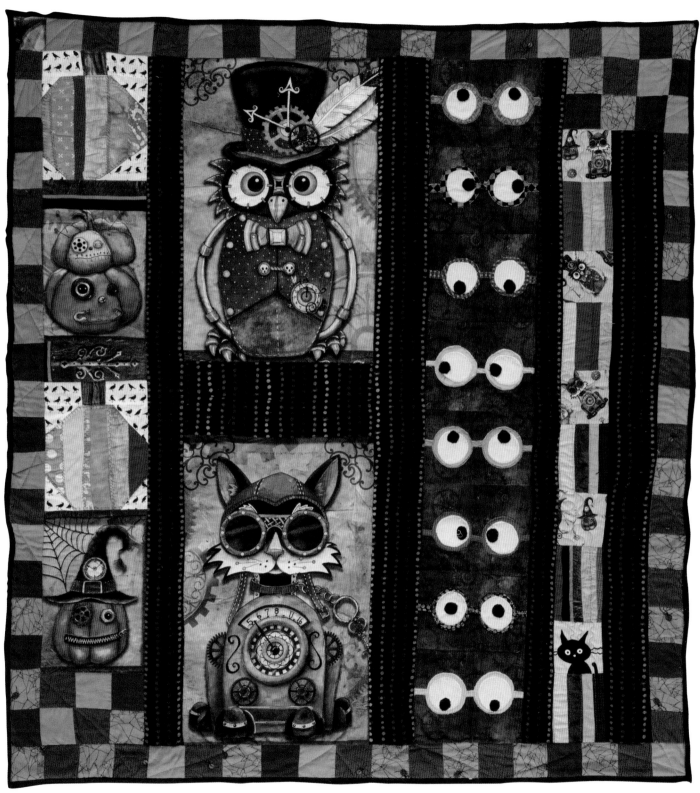

Steampunk Row 41˝ × 44˝ Row-by-row quilt by Kathleen Day
Steampunk Halloween panel by Desiree's Designs for QT Fabrics

Kathleen says, "Because of the layout for this panel, blocks were arranged in columns. The pieced and appliquéd goggles were inspired by whimsical eyewear on the two main characters."

Fabulous Fall Vibes 58˝ × 76˝ Row-by-row quilt by Pookie DeCocq
Maple Leaf Hills panel by Kris Lammers for Maywood Studio

Pookie confesses, "Quilting with panels never had appealed to me prior to Cyndi coming to our guild, giving a wonderful presentation, and offering a class. Cyndi has made a believer out of me and has opened up a new quilting genre that I truly love. Not only do I look forward to working with panels in the future; I am now enjoying and understanding how to design my own quilts. Game changer!"

Wildlife Row 77˝ × 90˝ Row-by-row quilt, designed by Marie Clanton and the author.
Pieced by Marie Clanton, quilted by the author

Marie notes, "This quilt is for my grandson and his new wife. Since they are ranchers in Colorado, I felt the wildlife panels were an appropriate choice. This quilt is actually a replacement for the first quilt I made him, as that one recently burned in a house fire. They lost everything except their animals in the fire!"

Baby's Besties 40″ × 52″ Repeated block quilt by the author
Happy Baby panel by Lorelie Harris for Loralie Designs

This fun panel by Lorelei Harris offered me another opportunity to feature panel images within a
repeated traditional block. I chose to use a variety of colors to create this bright and cheery baby quilt.

Beach Therapy 28″ × 40″ Montage quilt by Carolee Ellison
Beach Therapy panel by Deborah Edwards for Northcott Fabrics

Carolee recalls, "Growing up, I spent my summers at the Jersey shore. This panel reminded me of those times, and I really enjoyed brainstorming ideas for this quilt. I added other blocks that completed the memories and had fun embellishing it."

Surprise Party 54″ × 65″ Row-by-row quilt by the author
It's a Party! Panel by Loralie Harris for Lorelie Designs

I just love Lorelei Harris's whimsical ladies, and this party-themed panel brought a smile to my heart,
thinking of friends and our great times together.

Summer Memories 38˝ × 37˝ Montage quilt by Kim Pein
Beach Time by James Wiens for P&B Textiles

Kim comments, "This quilt was so much fun! I enjoyed the different appliqué pieces.
The quilt made me remember all the summers with my grandparents in Ocean City, Maryland."

X Marks the Spot 37½˝ × 37½˝ Montage quilt by the author
Enchanted Seas Pirate panel by Sillier Than Sally for P&B Textiles

What's more fun than hunting for buried treasure? This is a montage quilt with a whimsical seafaring and pirate theme. The panel offered me a lot of opportunity to play with featuring images in traditional blocks, highlighting the theme with related quilt blocks and embellishing in fun ways!

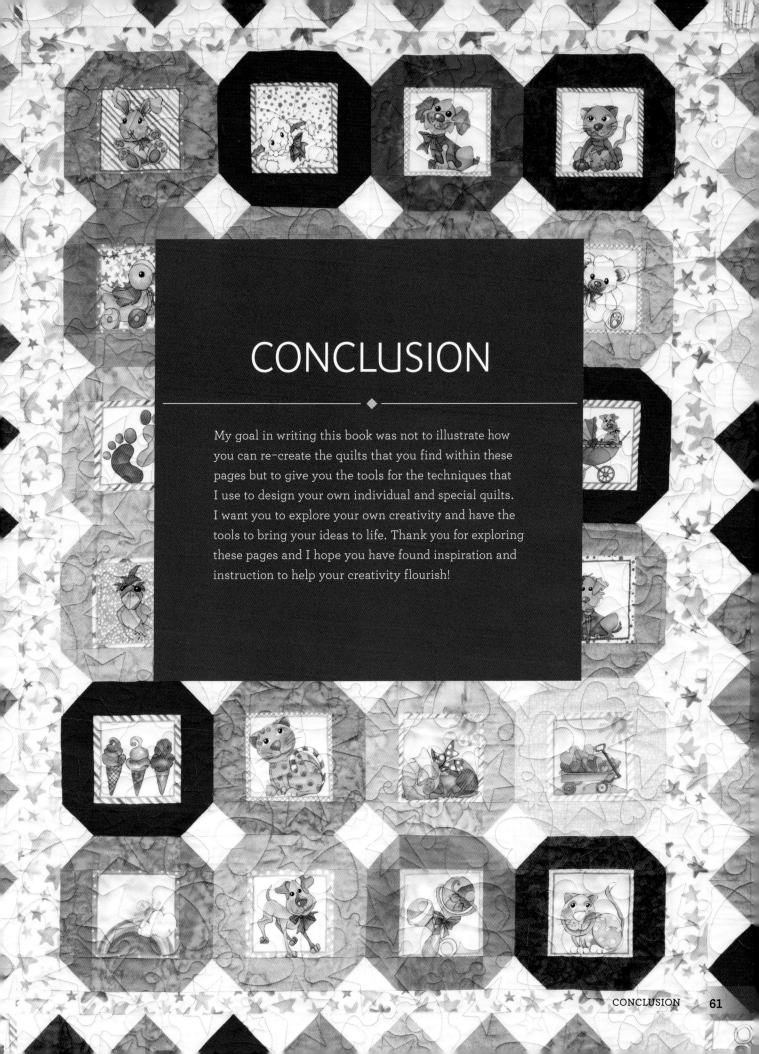

CONCLUSION

◆

My goal in writing this book was not to illustrate how
you can re-create the quilts that you find within these
pages but to give you the tools for the techniques that
I use to design your own individual and special quilts.
I want you to explore your own creativity and have the
tools to bring your ideas to life. Thank you for exploring
these pages and I hope you have found inspiration and
instruction to help your creativity flourish!

RESOURCES ❧

BLOCK LIBRARIES

The New Ladies' Art Company Quick & Easy Block Tool, by Connie Chunn

The New Quick & Easy Block Tool

Quilt Builder Card Deck

APPLIQUÉ PRIMERS

The Ultimate Appliqué Reference Tool, by Annie Smith

The Appliqué Book, by Casey York

EMBROIDERY GUIDES

Everyday Embroidery for Modern Stitchers, by Megan Eckman

Embroidery Stitching Handy Pocket Guide, by Christen Brown

ABOUT *the* AUTHOR

A much-sought-after quilting instructor, Cyndi endeavors to challenge students to embrace techniques that will enhance their ability to create unusual and unique designs. In her workshops, with detailed guidance, she encourages students to step out of their comfort zone and express themselves with confidence.

As an award-winning quilter and National Quilt Association Certified Teacher of the Year, Cyndi enjoys teaching throughout the United States and Canada and is known for her humorous and detailed teaching expertise.

Cyndi recently relocated to Virginia and is enjoying exploring the beaches and mountains of her new home state while continuing to delve into new and unusual ways to use panels. She operates her long-arm quilting business from her home studio and gets outdoors regularly with her dog, Strider.

Correspondence may be sent directly to Cyndi via email at cyndimcchesney@gmail.com.

Look for upcoming classes from Cyndi on C&T's teaching platform, Creative Spark!

Website www.cedarridgequilting.com

Facebook: /cedarridgequilting

CREATIVE SPARK
ONLINE LEARNING

Quilting courses to become an expert quilter...

From their studio to yours, Creative Spark instructors are teaching you how to create and become a master of your craft. So not only do you get a look inside their creative space, you also get to be a part of engaging courses that would typically be a one or multi-day workshop from the comfort of your home.

Creative Spark is not your one-size-fits-all online learning experience. We welcome you to be who you are, share, create, and belong.

Scan for a gift from us!